To:

Diane

From:

Lisa Lutz

Date:

Christmas 2000

The *Lord*
is my
Shepherd

AN INSPIRATIONAL BOOK OF HOPE

BOOKS

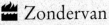

BOK3024

Contents

Psalm 23

The LORD is my Shepherd, I shall not be in
       want.
He makes me lie down in green pastures,
       he leads me beside quiet waters, he
       restores my soul.
He guides me in paths of righteousness for
       his name's sake.
Even though I walk through the valley of the
       shadow of death,
I will fear no evil, for you are with me;
       your rod and your staff, they comfort
       me.
You prepare a table before me in the pres-
       ence of my enemies.
You anoint my head with oil; my cup over-
       flows.
Surely goodness and love will follow me all
       the days of my life,
And I will dwell in the house of the LORD
       forever.

God Is
Our Source

Are you discouraged? Or shattered by an undeserved tragedy? Does it feel like you'll waste away from the monotony of meaningless days? Or like you can't go on?

Then it's time to praise the Lord.

Not for the problem, or for how you feel. But for *who he is.*

"Praise the Lord," wrote the psalmist. "And forget not all his benefits." God's children are entitled to his benefits, and these "special advantages" are wrapped up in his character. God is great. God is good. He is kind and merciful and powerful. This means that in our weaknesses and difficulties, we're heirs to his greatness, goodness, kindness, mercy and power. In fact, all of God's resources—all of his attributes—are available to us as we pass through the shadows.

So we can praise God for the unlimited resource of himself. He is our "very present" and stalwart help in times of trouble.

—Judith Couchman

God is our refuge and strength, an
ever–present help in trouble.

—Psalm 46:1

God is great, and therefore he will be
    sought;
He is good, and therefore He will be found.

—Anonymous

I will praise you, O LORD, with all my
    heart;
I will tell of your wonders.
I will be glad and rejoice in you;
I will sing praise to your name, O Most
    High.
The LORD is a refuge for the oppressed,
a stronghold in times of trouble.
Those who know your name will trust in
    you,
for you, LORD, have never forsaken those
    who seek you.

—Psalm 9:1–2, 9–10

Life—and praise—isn't always a feat of pure, simple gladness. Don't you find that in many situations you can experience both pleasant and unpleasant emotions? Like Paul, you can be "sorrowful, yet always rejoicing" (2 Corinthians 6:10). You can grow and suffer in this fallen world, yet you can learn to rejoice. You can learn to triumph in your hope, in your tribulations and the good things they produce in your life—and above all, in God Himself.

—Ruth Myers

Whatever troubles are weighing you down are not chains. They are featherweight when compared to the glory yet to come. With a sweep of a prayer and the praise of a child's heart, God can strip away any cobweb.

—Joni Eareckson Tada

Take a single promise of thy God; lean thy full weight upon it, and soon, very soon, thou wilt sing of the Lord because He hath dealt so lovingly with thee.

—Amy Carmichael

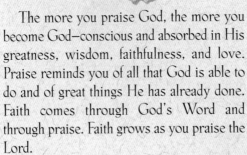

The more you praise God, the more you become God—conscious and absorbed in His greatness, wisdom, faithfulness, and love. Praise reminds you of all that God is able to do and of great things He has already done. Faith comes through God's Word and through praise. Faith grows as you praise the Lord.

Praise gives you the spirit of triumph and overcoming. Praise fires you with holy zeal. It lifts you above the battles to the perspective of God's throne. Praise cuts the enemy forces down to size. "If God is for us, who can be against us?" (Romans 8:31). "What can man do when God is with you?" (Psalm 118:6; Hebrews 13:6). "God's angel hosts with us are more than all who oppose us" (2 Kings 6:16).

—Wesley L. Duewel

God Forgives and Heals Us

I believe in the God who is not put off by
    our fiascoes.
I believe in the God who has an uncanny
    ability to bring good out of disaster.
I believe in the God who puts Humpty
    Dumpty back together again.

He is the God, in fact, whose "mercy
endureth forever." How many times have
we recited those words without absorbing
their meaning. His mercy has no cutoff. It
goes on... and on... and on....

It endures for the person who has made
an undeniable mistake in his life, whose
future has been torpedoed by one or more
fateful acts...

Divine mercy reaches as well to the
person who has not committed an overt act
of wrong, but has rather made a bad decision. It made sense enough at the time of
choosing, but with hindsight, it turns out to
have been tragic...

When dreams have been smashed, when
self–confidence has fled, when the future

goes blank, when even fellow Christians
shake their heads and look the other way—
is the Father's presence exhausted, too?

Let him speak for himself: "'I will restore
you to health and heal your wounds,'
declares the Lord, 'because you are called
an outcast, Zion for whom no one
cares.'"—Jeremiah 30:17

"I have seen his ways, but I will heal
him; I will guide him and restore comfort to
him."—Isaiah 57:18

—Dean Merrill

In place of our exhaustion and spiritual
fatigue, God will give us rest. All he asks is
that we come to him ... that we spend a
while thinking about him, meditating on
him, talking to him, listening in silence,
occupying ourselves with him—totally and
thoroughly lost in the hiding place of his
presence.

—Charles Swindoll

Jesus has forgiven us of all sin. He tells us to forgive others as Christ forgives us (Ephesians 4:32). If Jesus forgives you and He asks you to freely extend His forgiveness to those who offend you, is there any reason why you cannot forgive yourself?

You must be able to forgive yourself if you are to truly enjoy the liberation that God's forgiveness brings. Perhaps you have done something very bad. God forgives all sins; therefore, no sin should imprison you.

All forgiveness, including forgiving self, is founded on the cross. To deny yourself forgiveness is to try to obstruct God's holy love.

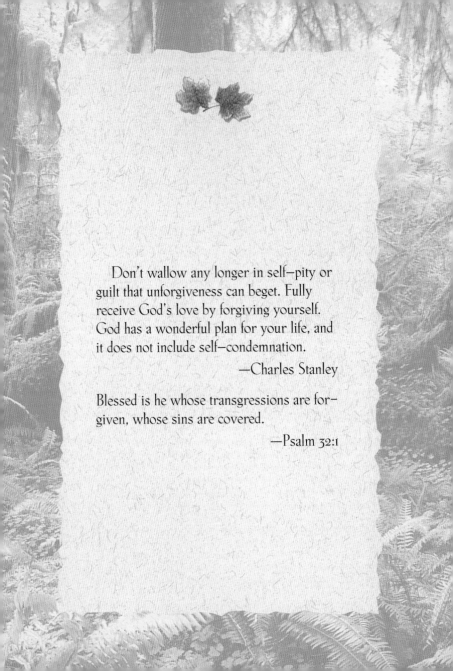

Don't wallow any longer in self—pity or guilt that unforgiveness can beget. Fully receive God's love by forgiving yourself. God has a wonderful plan for your life, and it does not include self—condemnation.

—Charles Stanley

Blessed is he whose transgressions are for-given, whose sins are covered.

—Psalm 32:1

God Restores Us

Redeeming is what God is into. He is
the finder of directionally challenged sheep,
the searcher of missing coins, the embracer
of foolish prodigal sons. His favorite
department is Lost and Found.

His love has no limits,
his grace has no measure,
his power has no boundaries
known unto men.

He redeems and redeems and redeems
and is present right now as you read these
words, and he longs to do for you what he
has done for countless rag dolls before you.
He is the God of the do—over; the Lord
of the second chance.

—John Ortberg

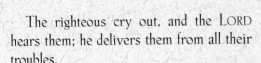

The righteous cry out, and the LORD hears them; he delivers them from all their troubles.

The LORD is close to the brokenhearted and saves those who are crushed in spirit.

A righteous man may have many troubles, but the LORD delivers him from them all; he protects all his bones, not one of them will be broken. Evil will slay the wicked; the foes of the righteous will be condemned. The LORD redeems his servants; no one will be condemned who takes refuge in him.

—Psalm 34:17–22

There's a Wideness
in God's Mercy

There's a wideness in God's mercy
Like the wideness of the sea;
There's a kindness in His justice
Which is more than liberty.
There is welcome for the sinner
And more graces for the good;
There is mercy with the Savior;
There is healing in His blood.
For the love of God is broader
Than the measure of man's mind;
And the heart of the Eternal
Is most wonderfully kind.
If our love were but more simple,
We should take Him at His word;
And our lives would be illumined
By the presence of our Lord.

—Frederick W. Faber

Although we are constantly failing and falling, yet doth He behold our faith as never failing, and ourselves as firm as Mount Zion, which cannot be moved, but standeth fast for ever. With never-changing fervency and tenderness of love, God beholds us chosen, redeemed, sanctified in Christ Jesus.

—Adolph Saphir

Fear not, for I have redeemed you; I have summoned you by name; you are mine.

—Isaiah 43:1

I have swept away your offenses like a cloud, your sins like the morning mist. Return to me, for I have redeemed you.

—Isaiah 44:22

My lips will shout for joy when I sing praise to you—I, whom you have redeemed.

—Psalm 71:23

O Lord, you took up my case; you redeemed my life.

—Lamentations 3:58

God Renews Us

Those who hope in the LORD will renew
their strength. They will soar on wings like
eagles; they will run and not grow weary,
they will walk and not be faint.

—Isaiah 40:31

The fact that Jesus came to earth where
he suffered and died does not remove pain
from our lives. But it does show that God
did not sit idly by and watch us suffer in
isolation. He became one of us. Thus, in
Jesus, God gives us an up-close and personal look at his response to human suffering. All our questions about God and
suffering should, in fact, be filtered through
what we know about Jesus...

When Jesus himself faced suffering, he
reacted much like any of us would. He
recoiled from it, asking three times if there
was any other way. There was no other
way, and then Jesus experienced, perhaps
for the first time, that most human sense of
abandonment: "My God, my God, why

have you forsaken me?" In the gospel accounts of Jesus' last night on earth, I detect a fierce struggle with fear, helplessness, and hope—the same frontiers all of us confront in our suffering.

The record of Jesus' life on earth should forever answer the question, How does God feel about our pain? In reply, God did not give us words or theories on the problem of pain. He gave us himself. A philosophy may explain difficult things, but has no power to change them. The gospel, the story of Jesus' life, promises change.

—Philip Yancey

O Lord, renew our spirits and draw our hearts unto Yourself, that our work may not be as a burden but a delight.

—Benjamin Jenks

Be transformed by the renewing of your mind.

—Romans 12:2

Because of his background, the apostle Paul knew all too well the frustration of knowing what to do without knowing how to do it. No doubt it was his own experience that made him sensitive to his readers' needs in this area. And so in one perfectly penned statement he summarized the key to consistent change: "by renewing the mind" (Romans 12:2).

Paul knew that our behavior is directly affected by the way we think. For real change to take place externally, there must first be a change in our thinking. Until we get involved in the process of renewing our minds, any behavioral change is going to be short-lived.

Renewing the mind is a little like refinishing furniture. It is a two–stage process. It involves taking off the old and replacing it with the new. The old is the lies you have learned to tell or were taught by those around you; it is the attitudes and ideas that have become a part of your thinking but do not reflect reality. The new is the truth. To renew your mind is to involve yourself in the process of allowing God to bring to the surface the lies you have mistakenly accepted and replace them with truth. To the degree that you do this, your behavior will be transformed.

—Charles Stanley

God is Just

He is the Rock,
his works are perfect:
and all His ways just.
A faithful God who
does no wrong, upright
and just is he.

—DEUTERONOMY 32:4

The modern idea that a judge should be cold and dispassionate has no place in the Bible. The biblical judge is expected to love justice and fair play and to loathe an ill—treatment of man by his fellow man. An unjust judge, one who has no interest in seeing right triumph over wrong, is by biblical standards a monstrosity. The Bible leaves us in no doubt that God loves right—eousness and hates iniquity, and that the ideal of a judge wholly identified with what is good and right is perfectly fulfilled in Him.

—J. I. Packer

Romantic love is blind to everything except what is lovable and lovely, but Christ's love sees us with terrible clarity and sees us whole. Christ's love so wishes our joy that it is ruthless against everything in us that diminishes our joy. The worst sentence Love can pass is that we behold the suffering which Love has endured for our sake, and that is also our acquittal. The justice and mercy of the judge are ultimately one.

—Frederick Buechner

God's justice is a bed where we
    Our anxious hearts may lay
And, weary with ourselves, may sleep
    Our discontent away.
For right is right, since God is God;
    And right the day must win;
To doubt would be disloyalty,
    To falter would be sin.

                    —Frederick William Faber

God Leads Us

Our caring Master offers what no other leader can. He not only sends His followers into the fray, but He also promises to go with them. And thus we may sing yet another song as we go: "No, never alone. No, never alone. He promised never to leave me, never to leave me alone."

God has always made this kind of commitment to His people. When Moses was sent to Egypt, he went with fear and trembling. But God said, "Now then go, and I, even I, will be with your mouth, and teach you what to say" (Exodus 4:12). Later, when Moses and the people stood trembling at the Red Sea with Pharaoh's army pressing upon them, God was there. His word to Moses was one of encouragement and promise.

—William Fletcher

Sing to God, sing praise to his name,
extol him who rides the clouds—
his name is the LORD—
and rejoice before him.

—*Psalm 68:4*

The LORD is my strength and my shield;
      my heart trusts in him, and I am
      helped.
My heart leaps for joy and I will give
      thanks to him in song.
The LORD is the strength of his people, a
      fortress of salvation for his anointed
      one.

—Psalm 28:7–8

I will lead the blind by ways they have not
    known,
   along unfamiliar paths I will guide them;
I will turn the darkness into light before
     them
   and make the rough places smooth.
These are the things I will do;
   I will not forsake them.

                —Isaiah 42:16

The LORD is my light and my salvation;
whom shall I fear? The LORD is the
strength of my life; of whom shall I be
afraid?

              —Psalm 27:1, KJV

God gives direction, changes our course, and guides even when we feel in the dark about what to do. Often when we think He's doing nothing to help us, the Lord is working in the blackness to shed light on our paths.

—Judith Couchman

He Leadeth Me

He leadeth me! O blessed thought!
O words with heav'nly comfort fraught!
Whate'er I do, where'er I be,
Still 'tis God's hand that leadeth me.
He leadeth me, He leadeth me;
By His own hand He leadeth me:
His faithful foll'wer I would be,
For by His hand He leadeth me.

—Joseph Gilmore

God Loves Us

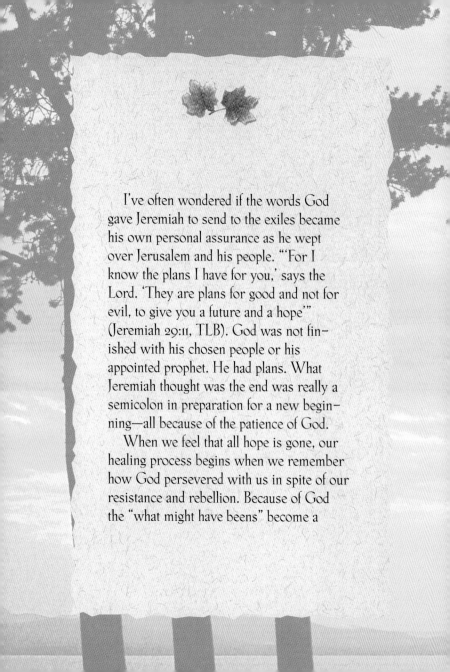

I've often wondered if the words God gave Jeremiah to send to the exiles became his own personal assurance as he wept over Jerusalem and his people. "'For I know the plans I have for you,' says the Lord. 'They are plans for good and not for evil, to give you a future and a hope'" (Jeremiah 29:11, TLB). God was not finished with his chosen people or his appointed prophet. He had plans. What Jeremiah thought was the end was really a semicolon in preparation for a new beginning—all because of the patience of God.

When we feel that all hope is gone, our healing process begins when we remember how God persevered with us in spite of our resistance and rebellion. Because of God the "what might have beens" become a

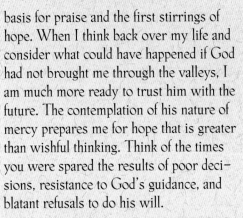

basis for praise and the first stirrings of hope. When I think back over my life and consider what could have happened if God had not brought me through the valleys, I am much more ready to trust him with the future. The contemplation of his nature of mercy prepares me for hope that is greater than wishful thinking. Think of the times you were spared the results of poor decisions, resistance to God's guidance, and blatant refusals to do his will.

—Lloyd J. Ogilvie

So long as we imagine it is we who have to look for God, we must often lose heart. But it is the other way about—He is looking for us.

—Simon Tugwell

Love is patient, love is kind.

—1 Corinthians 13:4

The Lord is not slow in keeping his promise, as some understand slowness. He is
patient with you, not wanting anyone to
perish, but everyone to come to repentance.

—2 Peter 3:9

The Lord Jehovah, God of the Covenant,
"is compassionate and gracious, slow to
anger, abounding in love" toward all who
fear Him. How truly, then, does this love
cast out fear of . . . condemnation.

—E. Calvin Beisner

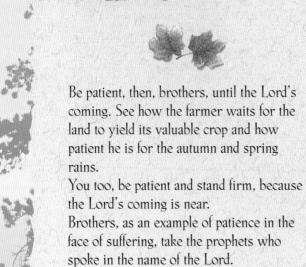

Be patient, then, brothers, until the Lord's
coming. See how the farmer waits for the
land to yield its valuable crop and how
patient he is for the autumn and spring
rains.
You too, be patient and stand firm, because
the Lord's coming is near.
Brothers, as an example of patience in the
face of suffering, take the prophets who
spoke in the name of the Lord.
As you know, we consider blessed those
who have persevered. You have heard of
Job's perseverance and have seen what the
Lord finally brought about. The Lord is full
of compassion and mercy.

—James 5:7–8, 10–11

God Offers
Us Grace

I grew up with the image of a mathematical God who weighed my good and bad deeds on a set of scales and always found me wanting. Somehow I missed the God of the Gospels, a God of mercy and generosity who keeps finding ways to shatter the relentless laws of ungrace. God tears up the mathematical tables and introduces the new math of grace, the most surprising, twisting, unexpected-ending word in the English language.

Grace makes its appearance in so many forms that I have trouble defining it. I am ready though, to attempt something like a definition of grace in relation to God. Grace means there is nothing we can do to make God love us more—no amount of spiritual calisthenics and renunciations, no amount of knowledge gained from seminaries and divinity schools, no amount of crusading on behalf of righteous causes. And grace means there is nothing we can do to make God love us less—no amount of racism or

pride ... or even murder. Grace means that God already loves us as much as an infinite God can possibly love.

—Philip Yancey

Restore us to yourself, O LORD, that we may return; renew our days as of old.

—Lamentations 5:21

Grace is seen in the story of Jesus. As I read the gospels, I am entranced by the simple and spontaneous way he accepted people heavy laden by their sense of being unacceptable. Accepted them, the publicans and sinners who were despised and rejected by those who thought they alone were acceptable, mired in the struggle nobody ever wins, the struggle to make themselves acceptable enough to be accepted by God.

When he met them he would simply say, without looking up their credentials or investigating their pasts, your sins are forgiven, you are accepted, go in peace.

—Lewis B. Smedes

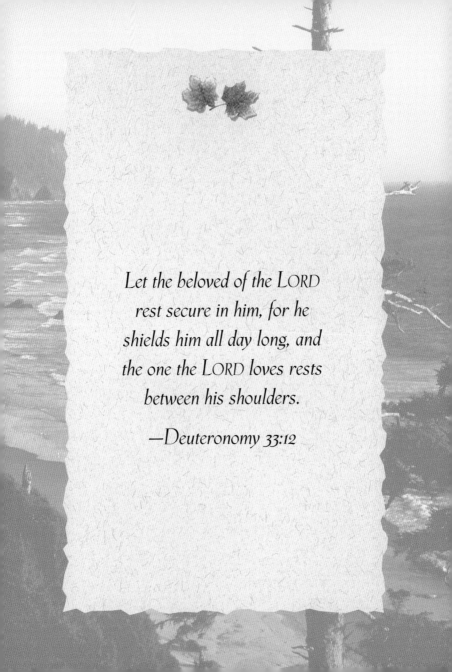

*Let the beloved of the L*ORD
rest secure in him, for he
shields him all day long, and
*the one the L*ORD *loves rests*
between his shoulders.

—*Deuteronomy 33:12*

God's Love
Is Endless

God knows the worst about us, the very worst, and still loves us.

We needn't worry about Him learning of some dastardly deed or habit or secret and then cutting us off. He already knows everything and His love remains infinite.

God also knows the very best about us, thoughts, words and deeds no other person knows about: how we've worked at study-ing His Word, what our true motives were when we were accused of wrong, what little deeds of kindness and goodness we've done around the house or work place just because they're right.

He knows it all. His love is a complete love, not naïve, not taken in, not hood-winked. He loves us each, as they say, "with His eyes wide open."

God desires that we rest in the knowl-edge of His knowledge. For there we can be sure that we are understood, accepted, and loved perfectly, completely and infinitely, without pause or regret.

—Mark R. Littleton

For I am convinced that neither death nor life, neither angels nor demons, neither the present nor the future, nor any powers, neither height nor depth, nor anything else in all creation, will be able to separate us from the love of God that is in Christ Jesus our Lord.

—Romans 8:38–39

There's nothing old or worn out about the love of God. His love has not yellowed with age. It is neither fragile nor ragged at the edges. God's love is as current now as it was a century ago, as fresh today as it will be tomorrow. Today, praise the Lord that He is the same, always loving, always merciful, and that with Him there is no shadow of turning.

—Joni Eareckson Tada

Christ's love is a love without angles; a love that asks nothing in return . . . this is the quality that redeems.

—David Wilkerson

He is a loving God. He loves you more dearly than your mother loves you, or your father, or your spouse. You are His child. So just get to know Him and trust His love. Then you will have that wholesome esteem for your own self that leads to having respect for all people.

—Norman Vincent Peale

In his love he clothes us, enfolds and embraces us; that tender love completely surrounds us, never to leave us.

—Julian of Norwich

I have loved you with an everlasting love; I have drawn you with loving–kindness.

—Jeremiah 31:3

O love that wilt not let me go,
I rest my weary soul in thee;
I give thee back the life I owe,
That in thine ocean depth its flow
May richer, fuller be.

—George Matheson

Give thanks to the LORD, for he is good. His love endures forever.

—Psalm 136:1

God Keeps Us From Evil

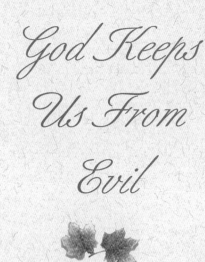

You may say, "If I could get rid of my sins, God would love me." But how can you get rid of it until you come to Him? He takes us into His own bosom, and He cleanses us from sin. He has shed His blood for you. He wants you, and He will redeem you today, if you will let Him.

—Dwight L. Moody

When we were overwhelmed by sins, you forgave our transgressions.

—Psalm 65:3

For I will forgive their wickedness and will remember their sins no more.

—Hebrews 8:12

And their sins and lawless acts will I remember no more.

—Hebrews 10:17

O Lord, we are not worthy to have a glimpse of heaven, and unable with our works to redeem ourselves from sin, death, the devil, and hell. For this we rejoice, praise and thank you, O God, that without price and out of pure grace you have granted us this boundless blessing in your dear Son through whom you take sin, death, and hell from us, and give to us all that belongs to him.

—Martin Luther

It is God who arms me with strength and makes my way perfect.

—Psalm 18:32

Because Jesus is Savior, He saves us from the penalty of sin. Because He is Lord, He, by His Holy Spirit, gives us power over sin as we daily walk with Him. And some future day He will take us to be with Himself, far from the very presence of sin (Hebrews 9:28). Only because Jesus is God and we have confessed Him as Savior and Lord, can He bestow and we receive these benefits, this blessed assurance and hope (Romans 10:9).

—Billy Graham

The Holy Spirit responds to the broken heart that reaches out, in faith, to lay hold of God's promises. He then imparts His divine nature to that empty vessel. A miraculous series of events begins to unfold. Suddenly there comes to the saint of God a renewed desire to confess, to yield to God's will, to become more like Jesus, to see things in the light of eternity, to experience a rush of surrender.

The Holy Spirit brings the yielded vessel around to God's way of thinking. We go after things we believe are good for us; we covet what is not ours. But God looks way down the road, and He knows what is best. Our ways and thoughts are not His ways or His thoughts. God will give His surrendered child something even better, if he lays down his own plan.

—David Wilkerson

We do not preach that Christ forgives people and then lets them live as before. We assert that the moment He gives the pardon of sin, He gives a new nature, too. The gospel is not merely a place where lepers are harbored, but where lepers are healed. "The Son of Man is come to seek and to save that which was lost."

—Charles H. Spurgeon

Blessed are those whose strength is in you.

—Psalm 84:5

So take courage! Christ has and will continue to win out over our present and future failures and problems. All He asks is that we give Him the glory. Then no one will gain the false impression that we did it ourselves for Christ and fall into the trap of trying to deal with their problems by their own effort. Paul was on target when he wrote, "We have this treasure in earthen vessels, that the excellence of the power may be of God and not of us" (2 Corinthians 4:7).

How do we then succeed when we've
 failed?

Admit our failure

Acknowledge our feelings of self-condem-
 nation
 and self-justification

Accept Christ's victory on the cross

Ask Him for forgiving peace for the past,
 a vision of His plan, and strengthening
 courage for the future
Press on!

      —Lloyd J. Ogilvie

God Has Compassion For Us

Nothing grips God's heart like the tortured cry of one of his children.

Watch what takes place in Psalm 18 after David says, "I cried to my God for help." David's plea reaches God's throne. God is roused.

"From his temple he heard my voice;
  my cry came before him, into his ears.
The earth trembled and quaked,
  and the foundations of the mountains
     shook . . .
He parted the heavens and came down . . .
He mounted the cherubim and flew;
  he soared on the wings of the wind . . .
He reached down . . . and took hold of me."

Our questions and cries powerfully move the Almighty. He parts heaven and shakes earth to respond. He reaches down. He takes hold.

Despair that rises in a direct and vertical line to God opens us up to change, real hope, and the possibility of seeing God as he really is, not as we want him to be. Once we give an inch, God will take a

mile. He'll take a million miles. He'll soar
on the wings of the wind from heaven to
here to show you who he is, to embrace
you with his love.

  —Joni Eareckson Tada and Steven Estes

  Yet this I call to mind and therefore I
have hope: Because of the LORD's great
love we are not consumed, for his compas-
sions never fail.
They are new every morning; great is your
   faithfulness.
I say to myself, "The LORD is my portion;
   therefore I will wait for him."
The LORD is good to those whose hope is
   in him, to the one who seeks him; it
   is good to wait quietly for the salvation of the LORD.

      —Lamentations 3:21–26

  God is full of compassion, and never
fails those who are afflicted and despised, if
they trust in Him alone.

       —Teresa of Avila

I keep thinking of all the people who cast despairing eyes toward the dark heavens and cry "Why?" And I imagine him [Jesus]. I imagine him listening. I picture his eyes misting and a pierced hand brushing away a tear. And although he may offer no answer, although he may solve no dilemma, although the question may freeze painfully in mid–air, he who also was once alone, understands.

—Max Lucado

Everything we will ever need to be all that God wants us to be has already been provided us by grace. The apostle Paul wrote, "And God is able to make all grace abound toward you, that you, always having all sufficiency in all things, may have abundance for every good work" (2 Corinthians 9:8).

And Paul continually referred to that abundance. In Ephesians 1:3, he said, "Blessed be the God and Father of our Lord Jesus Christ, who has blessed us with every spiritual blessing in heavenly places in Christ." It is important to observe that Paul is giving praise for blessings we already have, and these blessings are so comprehensive, they encompass everything.

Our challenge is not to ask God to bless us but to lay hold of what we already possess. God opened up an account in the Bank of Grace for you and me. In that account, He placed all the spiritual resources He would ever bestow upon us.

—Tony Evans

But he said to me, "My grace is sufficient for you, for my power is made perfect in weakness." Therefore I will boast all the more gladly about my weaknesses, so that Christ's power may rest on me.

—2 Corinthians 12:9

Jesus Christ,
guide us with your boundless compassion
and compel us with your perfect love
to love according to your will
in the truth . . .
that the truth may live in us
and we in the truth.

—Margaret Ebner

The LORD is gracious and righteous; our God is full of compassion.

—Psalm 116:5

O God, though our sins be seven, though our sins be seventy times seven, though our sins be more than the hairs of our head, yet give us grace in loving penitence to cast ourselves down into the depths of thy compassion.

—Christina Rossetti

You have not known the bottom rung of melancholia until loneliness pays you a lengthy visit. Peter Tchaikovsky knew. The composer wrote the following words in a minor key:

None but the lonely heart can feel my anguish....

God knows, my friend, and he does care. Please believe that! He not only knows and cares—he understands, he is touched, he is moved. Entering into every pulse of anguish, he longs to sustain and deliver us....

When we are lonely, we need an understanding friend. Jesus is the One who "sticks closer than a brother." When we are lonely, we need strength to keep putting one foot in front of the other—Jesus is the One "who strengthens me." When we are lonely, we need to lift our eyes off ourselves. Jesus, the "Founder and Finisher" of the life of faith, invites us to fix our eyes on him (Hebrews 12:1–3) and refuse to succumb.

God is a Specialist when the anguish is deep. His ability to heal the soul is profound . . . but only those who rely on his wounded Son will experience relief. Jesus answers Tchaikovsky with these words in a major key:

None but the trusting heart can feel My deliverance.

—Charles Swindoll

God Never Changes

Nothing can alter the character of God. In the course of a human life, tastes and outlook and temper may change radically: a kind, equable man may turn bitter and crotchety; a man of good–will may grow cynical and callous. But nothing of this sort happens to the Creator. He never becomes less truthful, or merciful, or just, or good, than He used to be. The character of God is today, and always will be, exactly what it was in Bible times.

—J. I. Packer

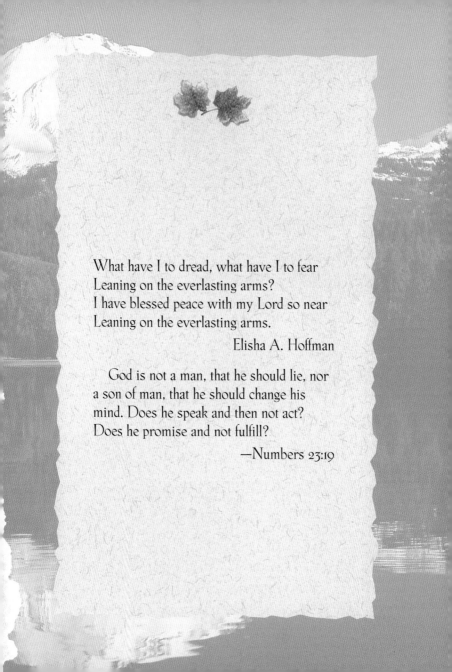

What have I to dread, what have I to fear
Leaning on the everlasting arms?
I have blessed peace with my Lord so near
Leaning on the everlasting arms.

Elisha A. Hoffman

God is not a man, that he should lie, nor
a son of man, that he should change his
mind. Does he speak and then not act?
Does he promise and not fulfill?

—Numbers 23:19

The Lord says:

Today I follow you wherever you go. I keep showing up, wherever you are, walking the roads you walk, sitting in the seat beside you as you drive, hovering close to you in a silent retreat center as you worry about courtroom scenes.

I do not go away. You must believe it. Believe it with all your heart: "He will never leave me." Say it to yourself when you awake to each new morning. Repeat it slowly throughout the day. Drift into sleep with the words on your lips.

And then, when you are as certain of My love and faithfulness as you are that the

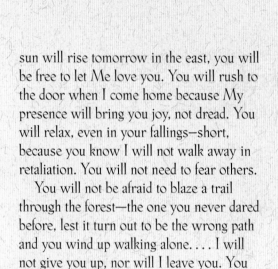

sun will rise tomorrow in the east, you will be free to let Me love you. You will rush to the door when I come home because My presence will bring you joy, not dread. You will relax, even in your fallings–short, because you know I will not walk away in retaliation. You will not need to fear others.

You will not be afraid to blaze a trail through the forest—the one you never dared before, lest it turn out to be the wrong path and you wind up walking alone.... I will not give you up, nor will I leave you. You belong to Me. I belong to you....

You are secure. You have nothing to lose. I'm with you always.

—Ruth Senter

God Is
in Control

My Life Is in Your Hands
Life can be so good
Life can be so hard
Never knowing what each day
Will bring to where you are.
Sometimes I forget
Sometimes I can't see
That whate'er comes my way
You'll be with me.
My life is in your hands
My heart is in your keeping.

—Kathy Troccoli

God is taking us on a great adventure. It will be out of our power and control. And it will be a ride like none we would have planned for ourselves. As we loosen our grip on the reins of our own lives, he is directing us down a trail we have never known.

—Dale Hanson Bourke

The only important decision we have to make is to live with God; He will make the rest.

—Anonymous

Dominion belongs to the LORD and he rules over the nations.

—Psalm 22:28

God Is Worthy of Our Praise

Praise the LORD, you his angels, you mighty ones who do his bidding, who obey his word. Praise the LORD, all his heavenly hosts, you his servants who do his will. Praise the LORD, all his works everywhere in his dominion. Praise the LORD, O my soul.

—Psalm 103:20–22

I'm never without hope
Not when my future is with you.
My life is in your hands
And though I may not
see it clearly
I will lift my voice and sing
Cause your love does
amazing things.
Lord, I know
My life is in your hands.

—Kathy Troccoli

Sources

Beisner, E. Calvin, *Psalms of Promise* (Colorado Springs: NavPress, 1988).

Bourke, Dale Hanson, *Turn Toward the Wind*, © 1995 by Dale Hanson Bourke, (Grand Rapids, MI: Zondervan Publishing House, 1995).

Buechner, Frederick, Excerpt from *Wishful Thinking: A Theological ABC.* © 1973 by Frederick Buechner, Reprinted by permission of HarperCollins Publishers, Inc.

Couchman, Judith, Excerpted from *His Gentle Voice*, © 1998 by Judith Couchman, Used by permission of Multnomah Publishers, Inc.

Cowman, Mrs. Charles E., *Streams in the Desert*, (Grand Rapids, MI: Zondervan Publishing House, 1965).

Duewel, Wesley L., *Mighty Prevailing Prayer*, (Grand Rapids, MI: Zondervan Publishing House, 1990). Used by permission of Duewel Literature Trust, Inc., Greenwood, IN.

Evans, Tony, *The Victorious Christian Life*, (Nashville: Thomas Nelson, 1994).

Ferguson, Sinclair B., *A Heart for God*, (Colorado Springs: NavPress, 1985).

Fletcher, William M., *The Triumph of Surrender*, (Colorado Springs: NavPress, 1987).

Frank, Jan, From *A Graceful Waiting*, © 1996 Jan Frank. Published by Servant Publications, Box 8617, Ann Arbor, Michigan, 48107. Used with permission.

Graham, Billy, *Unto the Hills*, © 1986, Word Publishing, Nashville, TN. All rights reserved.

Littleton, Mark R., *God Is!* (Lancaster, PA: Starburst, 1997).

Lucado, Max, Excerpted from *No Wonder They Call Him Savior*, © 1986 by Max Lucado, Used by permission of Multnomah Publishers, Inc.

Mead, Frank S., *The Encyclopedia of Religious Quotations* (Grand Rapids, MI: Fleming H. Revell, 1965).

Merrill, Dean, *The God Who Won't Let Go*, © 1981, 1998 by Dean Merrill (Grand

Rapids, MI: Zondervan Publishing House,
1998).

Moody, Dwight L., compiled by Judith
Couchman, *Only Trust Him* (Ann Arbor,
MI: Servant, 1998).

Myers, Ruth, Excerpted from *31 Days of
Praise*, © 1994, by Ruth Myers, Used by
permission of Multnomah Publishers, Inc.

Ogilvie, Lloyd J., *If God Cares, Why Do
I Still Have Problems?* © 1985. Word
Publishing, Nashville, TN. All rights
reserved. *Lord of the Impossible* (Nashville,
TN: Abingdon Press, 1984).

Ortberg, John, *Love Beyond Reason*, ©
1998 by John Ortberg (Grand Rapids, MI:
Zondervan Publishing House, 1998).

Packer, J.I, Taken from *Knowing God*, ©
1973 by J.I. Packer. Used with permission
from InterVarsity Press, P.O. Box 1400
Downers Grove, IL 60515, Reproduced by
permission of Hodder and Stoughton
Limited.

Peale, Norman Vincent, *In God We Trust*,
(Nashville, TN: Thomas Nelson, 1994).

Schuller, Robert H., *Life's Not Fair, But*

God is Good (Nashville, TN: Thomas Nelson, 1991).

Senter, Ruth, *Longing for Love* (Colorado Springs: NavPress, 1991).

Smedes, Lewis B., Excerpt from *Shame and Grace*, © 1993 by Lewis B. Smedes. Reprinted by permission of HarperCollins Publishers, Inc.

Spurgeon, Charles H., *For Me to Live is Christ*, (Ann Arbor, MI: Servant, 1998).

Stanley, Charles, *A Touch of His Freedom*, © 1991 by Charles F. Stanley, (Grand Rapids, MI: Zondervan Publishing House, 1991). *Enter His Gates* (Nashville, TN: Thomas Nelson, 1998).

Swindoll, Charles, *Encourage Me*, © 1982 by Charles R. Swindoll, Inc., (Grand Rapids, MI: Zondervan Publishing House, 1982), *Growing Strong in the Seasons of Life*, © 1983 by Charles R. Swindoll, Inc. (Grand Rapids, MI: Zondervan Publishing House: 1983).

Tada, Joni Eareckson, *Diamonds in the Dust*, © 1993 by Joni Eareckson Tada, (Grand Rapids, MI: Zondervan Publishing

House, 1993). *God's Precious Love,* © 1998 by Joni Eareckson Tada, (Grand Rapids, MI: Zondervan Publishing House, 1998), *When God Weeps,* © 1997 by Joni Eareckson Tada and Steven Estes, (Grand Rapids, MI: Zondervan Publishing House, 1997).

Troccoli, Kathy, *My Life is in Your Hands,* © 1997 by Kathy Trocolli, (Grand Rapids, MI: Zondervan Publishing House, 1997).

Wilkerson, David, *Have You Felt Like Giving Up Lately?* (Grand Rapids, MI: Fleming H. Revell, 1980).

Yancey, Philip, *What's So Amazing About Grace?* © 1997 by Philip D. Yancey (Grand Rapids, MI: Zondervan Publishing House, 1997), *Where is God When It Hurts?* © 1977, 1990 by Philip D. Yancey, (Grand Rapids, MI: Zondervan Publishing House, 1990).